D1519003

Salmon Migration

by Kari Schuetz

BLASTOFF!
3
READERS

BELLWETHER MEDIA • MINNEAPOLIS, MN

Note to Librarians, Teachers, and Parents:

Blastoff! Readers are carefully developed by literacy experts and combine standards-based content with developmentally appropriate text.

Level 1 provides the most support through repetition of high-frequency words, light text, predictable sentence patterns, and strong visual support.

Level 2 offers early readers a bit more challenge through varied simple sentences, increased text load, and less repetition of high-frequency words.

Level 3 advances early-fluent readers toward fluency through increased text and concept load, less reliance on visuals, longer sentences, and more literary language.

Level 4 builds reading stamina by providing more text per page, increased use of punctuation, greater variation in sentence patterns, and increasingly challenging vocabulary.

Level 5 encourages children to move from "learning to read" to "reading to learn" by providing even more text, varied writing styles, and less familiar topics.

Whichever book is right for your reader, Blastoff! Readers are the perfect books to build confidence and encourage a love of reading that will last a lifetime!

This edition first published in 2019 by Bellwether Media, Inc.

No part of this publication may be reproduced in whole or in part without written permission of the publisher. For information regarding permission, write to Bellwether Media, Inc., Attention: Permissions Department, 6012 Blue Circle Drive, Minnetonka, MN 55343.

Library of Congress Cataloging-in-Publication Data

Names: Schuetz, Kari, author.
Title: Salmon Migration / by Kari Schuetz.
Description: Minneapolis, MN : Bellwether Media, Inc., 2019. | Series:
   Blastoff! Readers. Animals on the Move | Audience: Age 5-8. | Audience:
   Grade K to 3. | Includes bibliographical references and index.
Identifiers: LCCN 2018000202 (print) | LCCN 2018005326 (ebook) | ISBN
   9781626178199 (hardcover : alk. paper) | ISBN 9781681035604 (ebook)
Subjects: LCSH: Salmon--Migration--Juvenile literature.
Classification: LCC QL638.S2 (ebook) | LCC QL638.S2 S298 2019 (print) | DDC 597.5/61568--dc23
LC record available at https://lccn.loc.gov/2018000202

Editor: Paige V. Polinsky   Designer: Jeffrey Kollock

Printed in the United States of America, North Mankato, MN

Table of Contents

Salmon

Salmon are strong swimmers. These powerful fish **migrate** through both **saltwater** and **freshwater**.

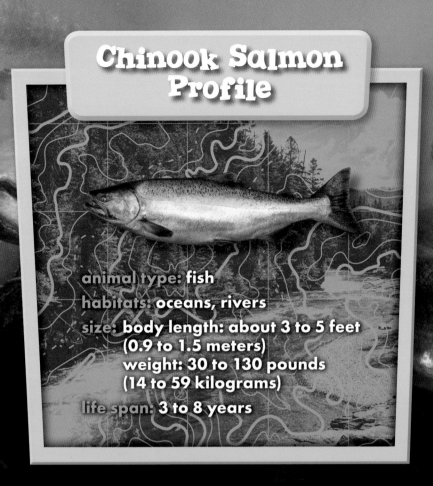

Chinook Salmon Profile

animal type: fish

habitats: oceans, rivers

size: body length: about 3 to 5 feet (0.9 to 1.5 meters)
weight: 30 to 130 pounds (14 to 59 kilograms)

life span: 3 to 8 years

They are famous for leaving the ocean to **spawn** far away in rivers. For Chinook salmon, the trip covers thousands of miles!

Salmon **adapt** to travel from oceans to rivers. Their **gills** change to handle freshwater.

gills

Their scales change, too.
The shiny silver fish turn bright
colors. This shows other salmon
they are ready to spawn.

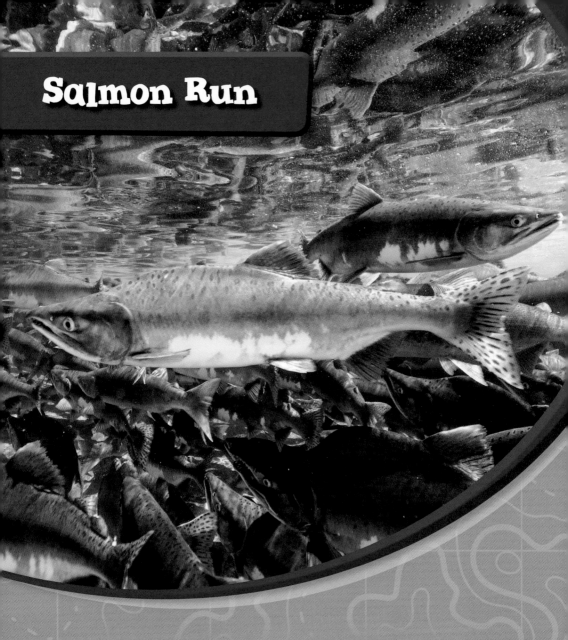

Salmon Run

Salmon spend most of their lives in the ocean. Yet every summer and fall, many must leave their saltwater homes.

These fish swim toward rivers to spawn. Their journey is called the salmon run.

Salmon do not eat while they migrate. They must fill up on smaller fish before leaving the ocean.

Then they wait in **estuaries**. This helps their bodies adapt to less salty water.

estuary

ocean

Chinook Salmon Departure

mode of travel: swimming

leaving
June: Bering Sea

arriving
August:
Yukon River

Strong Swimmers

Salmon swim upstream in large groups. They must fight rushing water and jump up waterfalls.

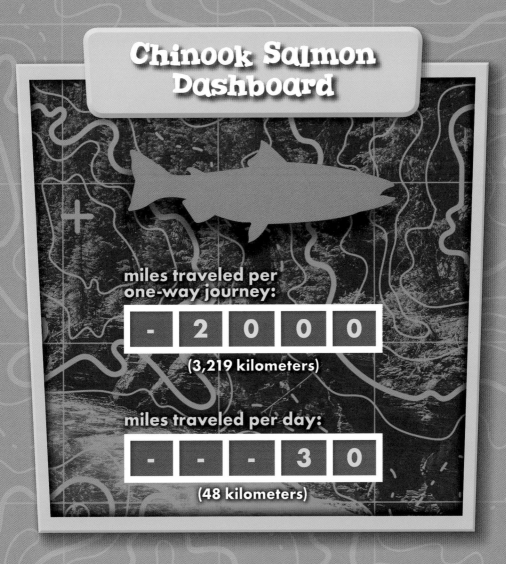

Chinook Salmon Dashboard

miles traveled per one-way journey:

-	2	0	0	0

(3,219 kilometers)

miles traveled per day:

-	-	-	3	0

(48 kilometers)

The fish follow their noses along the way. Smell guides them back to where they were born.

Bering
Sea

Alaska

Pacific
Ocean

N
W E
S

Dams block some salmon on
their river journey. But some dams
have fish ladders. These are pools
of water salmon can climb.

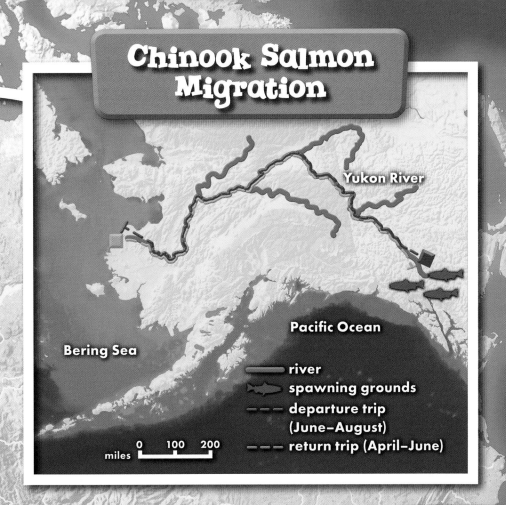

Chinook Salmon Migration

Yukon River

Pacific Ocean

Bering Sea

river

spawning grounds

- - - departure trip
(June–August)

- - - return trip (April–June)

miles 0 100 200

North America

Predators also make the trip difficult. Hungry bears snap up salmon for dinner.

15

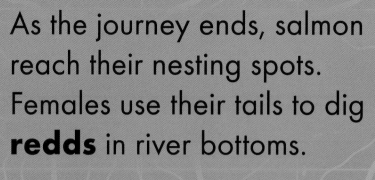

As the journey ends, salmon reach their nesting spots. Females use their tails to dig **redds** in river bottoms.

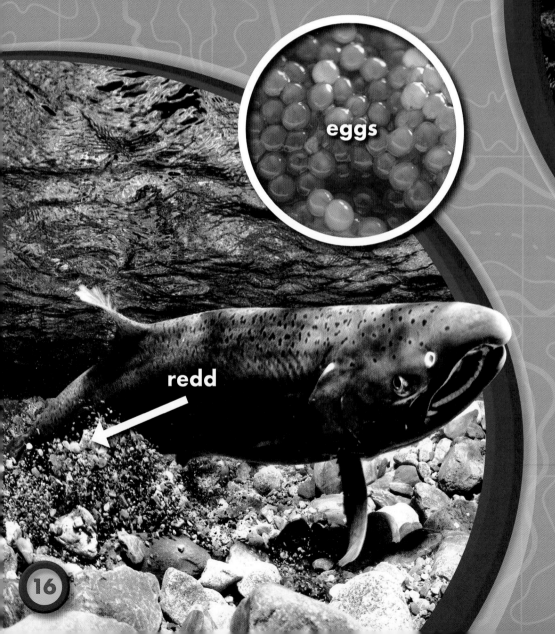

eggs

redd

Each redd will hold up to one thousand eggs. Males compete to spawn with the females.

To the Ocean

Most adult salmon die after spawning. Their babies often **hatch** from eggs around spring.

Some types of salmon swim downstream just months after hatching. Others take years to leave their freshwater homes.

Young travelers
are called **smolts**.
They migrate to the
ocean, where there
is plenty to eat.

There they stay to feed
and grow into adults.
Then these salmon
repeat their parents'
river run!

smolts

Chinook Salmon Smolt Return

mode of travel: swimming

arriving June: Bering Sea

leaving April: Yukon River

Glossary

adapt—to change in order to survive

dams—walls built across rivers to stop or redirect flowing water

estuaries—places where saltwater and freshwater mix

freshwater—water that is not salty; freshwater fills rivers, lakes, and ponds.

gills—the organs through which salmon breathe

hatch—to break out of an egg

migrate—to travel from one place to another, often with the seasons

predators—animals that hunt other animals for food

redds—salmon nests

saltwater—water that is salty; saltwater fills oceans and seas.

smolts—young adult salmon

spawn—to produce a great number of young

To Learn More

AT THE LIBRARY

Best, B.J. *Salmon*. New York, N.Y.: Cavendish Square Publishing, 2017.

Fishman, Jon M. *The Salmon's Journey*. Minneapolis, Minn.: Lerner Publications, 2018.

Hansen, Grace. *Salmon Migration*. Minneapolis, Minn.: ABDO Kids, 2017.

ON THE WEB
Learning more about salmon migration is as easy as 1, 2, 3.

1. Go to www.factsurfer.com.

2. Enter "salmon migration" into the search box.

3. Click the "Surf" button and you will see a list of related web sites.

With factsurfer.com, finding more information is just a click away.

Index

The images in this book are reproduced through the courtesy of: Design Pics Inc/ Alamy, front cover (salmon); Damsea, front cover (riverbed, waterline/blur); Rusla Ruseyn, front cover (mountains/sky/top of river); Maks Ershov, front cover (gradient map); Mark Conlin/ Alamy, pp. 4-5; Gennady Teplitskiy, p. 5; WorldFoto/ Alamy, p. 6; Beat J Korner, p. 9; Jairo Rene Leiva, p. 10; National Geographic Creative/ Alamy, pp. 10-11; Mksimilian, p. 12; m. uptegrove, p. 16 (top); Thomas Kline/ Getty, pp. 16 (bottom), 19; Thomas Kline/ SuperStock, p. 17; Zykov_Vladimir, p. 18; Mark Conlin/ SuperStock, p. 20; Supercaliphotolistic, p. 21.